E
RAU
Rau, Dana Meachen
My Special Space

BA
10649425

$9.39

103644 EN
My Special Space

Rau, Dana Meachen
ATOS BL 1.6
Points: 0.5   LG

My **Special** Space

Written by Dana Meachen Rau

Illustrated by Julie J. Kim

Children's Press®
A Division of Scholastic Inc.
New York • Toronto • London • Auckland • Sydney
Mexico City • New Delhi • Hong Kong
Danbury, Connecticut

For Chris, Charlie, and Allison,
who let me have a special space,
and often get invited in
—D.M.R.

For my greatest blessing…my family
—J.J.K.

Reading Consultants

Linda Cornwell
Literacy Specialist

Katharine A. Kane
Education Consultant
(Retired, San Diego County Office of Education
and San Diego State University)

Library of Congress Cataloging-in-Publication Data

Rau, Dana Meachen, 1971-
  My special space / written by Dana Meachen Rau ;
illustrated by Julie J. Kim.- 1st American ed.
       p. cm. — (Rookie reader)
Summary: A girl describes the hideaway in her closet where she goes when
she wants to spend time by herself.
  ISBN 0-516-22881-1 (lib. bdg.)   0-516-27788-X (pbk.)
  [1. Solitude—Fiction. 2. Clothes closets—Fiction. 3. Stories in rhyme.]
I. Kim, Julie J., 1973- ill. II. Title. III. Series.
  PZ8.3.R232My 2003
  [E]—dc21

                          2003003887

CHILDREN'S PRESS, and A ROOKIE READER®, and associated logos are trademarks and or
registered trademarks of Scholastic Library Publishing. SCHOLASTIC and associated logos
are trademarks and or registered trademarks of Scholastic Inc.
1 2 3 4 5 6 7 8 9 10 R 12 11 10 09 08 07 06 05 04 03

My mother has a special space.
She likes her purple chair.

4

My father likes the table.
He reads the paper there.

My brother likes the tree house.

My sister likes the floor.

My pets have special spaces
behind the kitchen door.

Hoover-Wood
Elementary School

11

My special space is somewhere
I can be all by myself.

I have pillows there,
my blanket, too,
and drawings on the shelf.

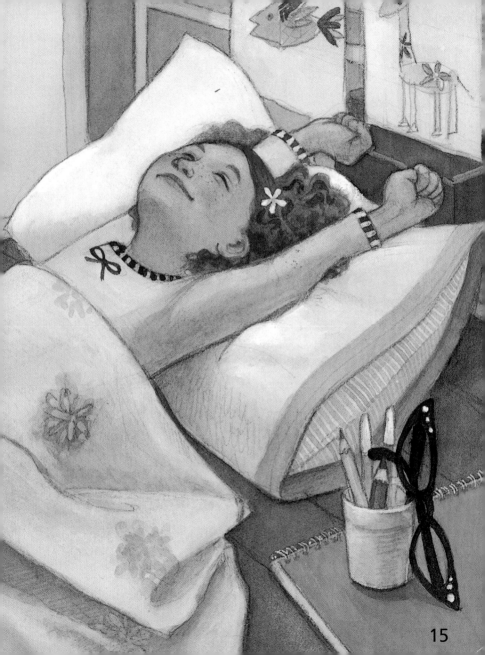

Sometimes I like to daydream.

Sometimes I read my books.

Sometimes I do my homework or practice funny looks.

Hoover-Wood
Elementary School

21

Sometimes I play with puzzles.

Sometimes I sing off-key.

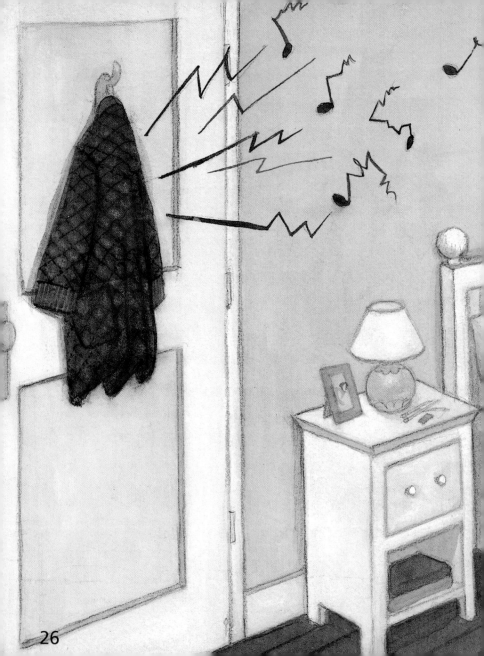

It's okay to make mistakes
because it's only me.

But sometimes it's too quiet
in my secret hiding place.